Amazing Spiders

Lycosa tarentula

Amazing Spiders

by Claudia Schnieper/photographs by Max Meier

A Carolrhoda Nature Watch Book

Carolrhoda Books, Inc./Minneapolis

Thanks to Bruce Cutler, Ph.D,
for his assistance with this book.

A note on the names of spiders appears on page 44.

This edition of this book is available in two bindings:
Library binding by Carolrhoda Books, Inc.
Soft cover by First Avenue Editions
241 First Avenue North
Minneapolis, Minnesota 55401

This edition first published 1989 by Carolrhoda Books, Inc.
Original edition copyright © 1986 by Kinderbuchverlag Reich Luzern
AG, Lucerne, Switzerland, under the title SPINNEN: FALLENSTELLER
IM SEIDENEN NETZ. Translated from the German by Betmar
Languages. Adapted by Carolrhoda Books, Inc.
All additional material supplied for this edition ©1989 by
Carolrhoda Books, Inc.

LIBRARY OF CONGRESS CATALOGING-IN-PUBLICATION DATA

Schnieper, Claudia.
 ⌈Spinnen. English⌉
 Amazing spiders/by Claudia Schnieper: photographs by Max Meier.
   p.   cm.
 Translation of: Spinnen.
 "A Carolrhoda nature watch book."
 Includes index.
 Summary: Introduces the varieties, appearance, behavior, and life
cycles of spiders.
   ISBN 0-87614-342-7 (lib. bdg.)
   ISBN 0-87614-518-7 (pbk.)
   1. Spiders—Juvenile literature. ⌈1. Spiders.⌉ I. Meier, Max,
ill. II. Title.
QL458.4.S3613   1989
595.4′4—dc19   88-39199
                                                   CIP
Manufactured in the United States of America   AC

 2 3 4 5 6 7 8 9 10 99 98 97 96 95 94 93 92 91 90 89

Araneus diadematus has a body length of about ½ to ¾ inch (12 to 19 millimeters).

Are you afraid of spiders? If a spider sat down beside you, would you, like Miss Muffet, be frightened away? Many people have a fear of spiders, yet most of these little creatures are completely harmless. There are only a few kinds of spiders in the world with poison strong enough to affect humans.

Perhaps you fear spiders because they seem "creepy" to you. They scurry over the ground on long, hairy legs or sit motionless for hours in the middle of a web. Around the house, you often see spiders in the corners of attics or basements. Why are they hiding in these dark places? What kind of animals are spiders, and why do they behave in such mysterious ways?

One of the most important things to know about spiders is that they are not insects. Spiders have eight legs, while insects have only six. Most insects have wings and antennae, but spiders have neither. Spiders are **arachnids** (uh-RACK-nids), members of a scientific group that also includes scorpions, daddy longlegs, mites, and ticks.

There are at least 30,000 known **species** (SPEE-sheez), or kinds, of spiders in the world. They live in all sorts of places: in hot deserts and on cold mountaintops, in meadows, gardens, caves, and people's houses. Some spiders are smaller than the head of a pin, while others are almost as big as a dinner plate.

The habits of spiders are also quite different. Many spiders weave compli-cated webs made out of silk. Some web-weaving spiders make round **orb webs** like the one shown on the opposite page. Other spiders produce webs shaped like sheets, funnels, or bowls.

Web-weaving spiders use their webs to trap insects, but other spiders get their food in different ways. Hunters like the wolf spider and the jumping spider move around in search of **prey.** Brightly colored crab spiders hide themselves in flowers and seize bees that come to drink nectar.

Despite their different habits, all spiders have some things in common. They are all **predators** that kill and eat other animals. All kinds of spiders also produce silk and use it as an important part of their lives.

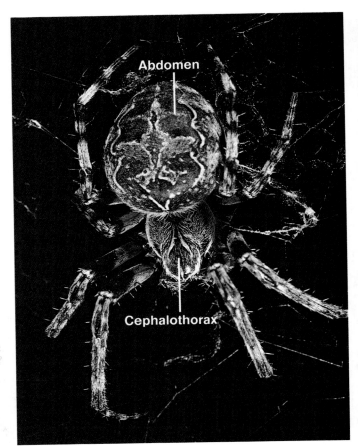

Nuctenea sclopetaria. Body length about ⅜ to ½ inch (9 to 12 mm)

A spider's silk is produced by silk glands located in its **abdomen**, the back part of the body. The silk thread comes out from the rear of the abdomen through tubes known as **spinnerets** (SPIN-uh-rehts). In the photograph on the upper right, you can see a silk thread coming out of one of a spider's spinnerets.

Spiders make several kinds of silk. Some silk is sticky, while other kinds are dry. Spider silk is produced as a liquid, but it hardens when exposed to air.

The front part of a spider's body is the **cephalothorax** (sef-uh-luh-THOR-acks). Within this section are located the stomach and the brain. All eight of a spider's legs are connected to the cephalothorax. The legs are covered with hairs that serve as sense organs. They pick up vibrations and smells from the air. All spiders have at least two tiny claws at the end of each leg.

A spider's head is the front part of its cephalothorax. On the head are

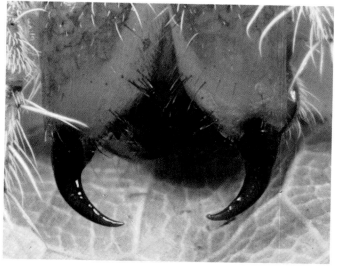

located the eyes—usually eight in most spiders, but sometimes six, four, or two.

Below a spider's eyes and near its mouth are two important body parts called **chelicerae** (kuh-LIS-uh-ree). These small organs are used to grab and kill prey. Each chelicera has a sharp, hollow fang at its end. Poison flows through these fangs and into the prey's body. The photograph on the left shows the chelicerae and fangs of a spider.

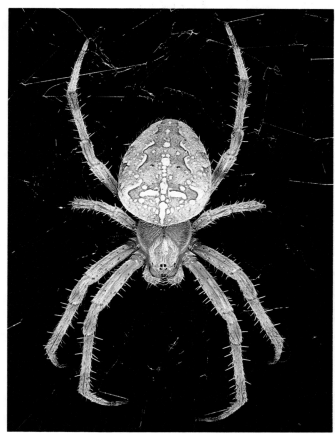

The spider shown on these two pages is a member of the large group commonly known as garden spiders, found in North America and many other parts of the world. (The spider's scientific name is *Araneus diadematus*.) Garden spiders are famous for the orb webs that they weave. If you get up early in the morning, you may see one of these round webs in your garden or yard, its threads sparkling with dew. How does the garden spider produce such a beautiful and complicated structure?

A garden spider does not have to "learn" how to weave an orb web. Every spider is born with the **instinct** to build exactly the same kind of web made by all spiders of its species. It performs this amazing task using only its mouth, its eight legs, and the silk threads produced in its body.

An orb-web weaver begins its work by first making a **bridge thread**. Perched on a twig or branch, the spider releases a thread of silk from a spinneret and lets the wind carry it away (1). When the sticky thread catches on another twig, the spider crawls across it, adding other

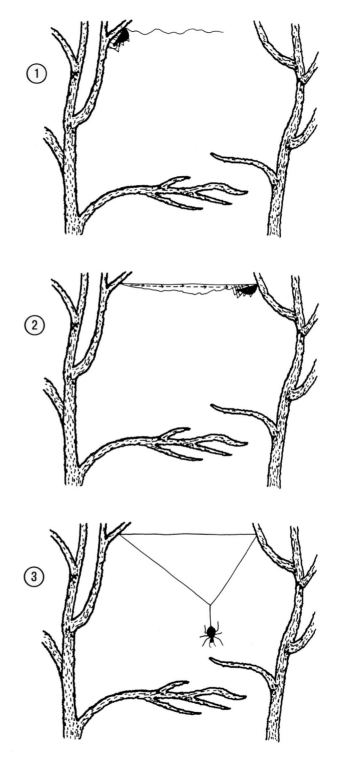

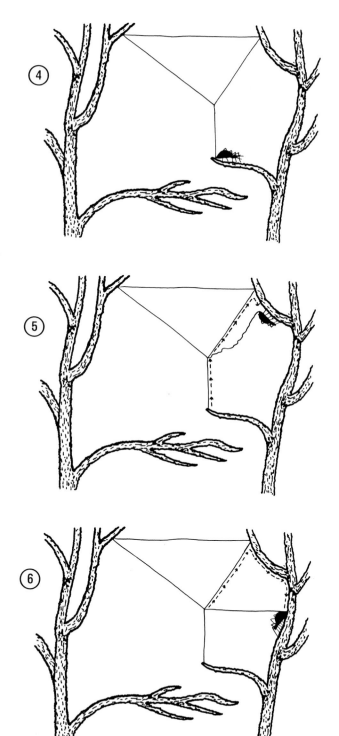

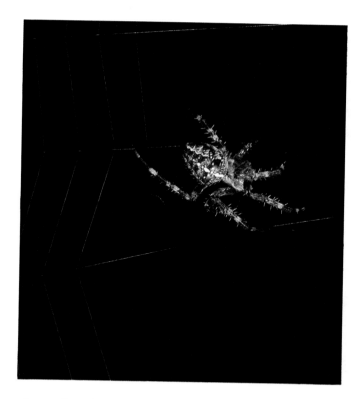

threads that strengthen this basic part of the web.

The next step is making the first "spokes" of the circular web. To do this, the spider crawls across the bridge trailing a loose thread behind it (2). After attaching the end of the thread to the opposite support, the spider moves to its center and starts a new thread (3). Dropping down on this thread to another support point, the spider pulls the thread tight and attaches it (4). The web now has a Y-shaped frame that can be used in making the other spokes and support lines (5, 6).

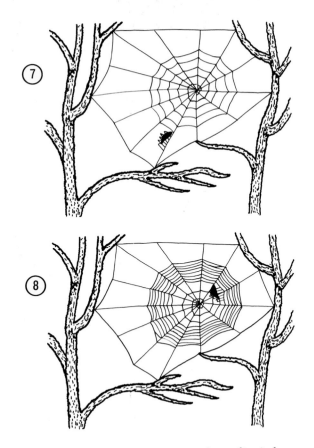

After the garden spider finishes the spokes of its web, it is ready to make the spiral part. First it creates a temporary spiral that will support the web until the permanent spiral is built. Starting at the center of the web, the spider moves outward in a circle, attaching a thread of dry silk to the spokes (7).

When the spider has completed the temporary spiral, it starts back toward the center of the web. As the spider travels back over the spiral, it eats the temporary thread. At the same time, it produces a thread of sticky silk that will make up the permanent spiral. The spider carefully attaches the thread to each spoke (8). It often leaves a space around the center of the web, where it will sit waiting for visitors (above right). When the web is completed, the sticky, tightly woven spiral will serve as a trap, catching insects that fly into it.

Many orb-web weavers make new webs every night, usually using the old bridge threads. Other spiders repair damaged webs by replacing threads and patching up holes.

Argiope species. Body length about 1 inch (25 mm)

Some kinds of orb-web spiders put special structures in the centers of their webs. *Argiope*, the beautiful yellow-and-black spider shown on the opposite page, weaves shiny ribbons of silk into its web (above). This pattern may help to hide the spider as it waits in the center of the web. Or it may serve a very different purpose by making the web easy to see. Some scientists believe that these bright areas of silk help birds to spot a spider web and to avoid flying into it.

17

Orb webs are not the only kinds of silken insect traps made by spiders. Some spiders make horizontal **sheet webs** close to the ground. A sheet web often has lines of silk that criss-cross above it. Insects bounce off these lines and get tangled in the sheet below. *Crytophora*, shown below, is one of several kinds of spiders that make sheet webs.

Other spiders build **funnel webs**.

Crytophora species. Body length about ⅝ inch (about 15 mm)

Tegenaria atrica. Body length about ½ inch (12 mm)

This kind of web has a flat sheet of silk at the top. The bottom of the web is shaped like a funnel, wide at one end and narrow at the other. Within the narrow part of the funnel, the spider hides while it waits for prey.

Many funnel-web spiders make their webs in tall grass. Others, like *Tegenaria* (above), build them in dark corners of people's houses.

Argiope bruennichi.
Body length about 1 inch (25 mm)

Whether they are shaped like orbs, sheets, or funnels, all spider webs are designed to trap insects. A web-weaving spider does not have to go out and look for food. It simply waits for the food to come to it.

Some orb-web weavers, like the one on the opposite page, wait at the center of their web. Others sit at the edge of the web with their legs touching a **signal thread.**

Most web-weaving spiders have poor eyesight, but the vibration of the web tells them when an insect has entered the trap. The spider rushes to the spot, seizes the prey, and begins to wrap it in silk threads. Using its front legs to turn the insect around and around, the spider wraps the silk with its back legs (above right).

After the packaging is finished, the spider pierces the insect's body with its fangs and injects poison. The poison kills the insect or paralyzes it. Then the spider carries the prey to its "dining room" and begins to eat. If the spider is not hungry, it may hang the insect in the web and save it for another meal.

Thomisus onustus. Body length about ⅓ inch (10 mm)

Spiders that don't make webs have different ways of getting their food. Crab spiders (above) sit quietly on flowers, waiting to ambush insects. These beautiful spiders wear colors that match the petals and centers of flowers. Camouflaged in this way, they are very hard to see. Bees and butterflies in search of nectar often become the prey of well-hidden crab spiders. These hunters have a very powerful poison and can kill insects much larger than themselves.

Jumping spiders are active hunters that chase prey. These little spiders, like the one shown on this page, have very good eyesight. They are able to spot insects from fairly far away. A jumping spider creeps up on its prey and then pounces with a quick jump. In case the predator misses its target, a silk **dragline** keeps it from falling. Like crab spiders, jumping spiders use a quick-acting poison to kill the insects that provide their food.

Philaeus chrysops. Body length ¼ to ½ inch (6 to 12 mm)

Araneus diadematus

Spiders cannot chew or swallow their food. They eat only liquids, but they are able to turn an insect like this fly into a kind of soup. Orb-web spiders (right) have teeth on their chelicerae with which they crush the prey's body. Then they pour on digestive juices that turn the soft parts of the body into a liquid. The spider sucks the liquid up with its mouth. When it is done, all that is left is a crushed mass of hard body parts (lower right).

Crab spiders and some other species do not have teeth on their chelicerae. They inject digestive juices into an insect's body through the holes made by their fangs. Then they suck out the "soup" through the same holes. After one of these spiders has eaten, its prey looks almost undamaged, but it is only a hollow shell.

Argiope bruennichi

Spiders spend much of their time catching food. They try to kill and eat almost any small creature that comes near them, including other spiders. When it is time for mating, however, male and female spiders have to meet for peaceful purposes.

In order to mate, a male spider must first find a female of his species. Then he must convince her that he is not just another meal. Male spiders use different methods to achieve this goal. A male web-weaving spider like *Argiope* (opposite right) approaches the web of a female and gently plucks the threads with his claws. He uses an even, steady rhythm very different from the jerky movements of an insect caught in the web. This signal lets the large female (left) know that a male of her species has come looking for a mate.

Because they have good eyesight, hunting spiders can use visual signals in mating. A male wolf spider waves his hairy front legs like a human signaling with flags. Male jumping spiders do special "dances" to tell females who they are and what they want.

Sometimes a female spider ignores the message and eats the male. Frequently,

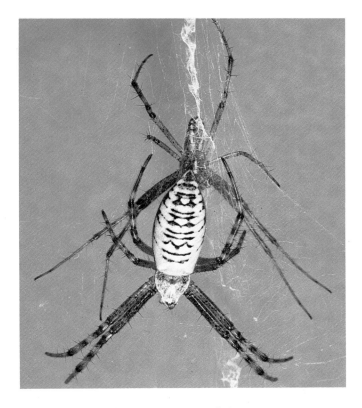

however, she accepts him as a mate (above). Mating in spiders is different than mating in many other animals. Before a male spider goes to look for a mate, he makes a small web and deposits **sperm** (male reproductive cells) on it. Then he takes up the sperm in two special organs called **palps,** located near his mouth. (The photograph on the next page shows the palps of a male spider.) When a male mates with a female, he uses his palps to put the sperm into her body through her reproductive opening.

27

Palps

The spiders shown on these two pages belong to the species *Nuctenea sclopetaria.*

After mating, most male and female spiders separate. Sometimes the female eats her partner before he gets away, but this is not very common.

The female's next big job is laying her eggs. Some kinds of spiders lay only two or three eggs at one time, while others produce several hundred. As the eggs are laid, they are fertilized by the male sperm cells stored in the female's body.

Almost all female spiders protect their eggs by wrapping them in silk. A female usually makes a silk platform on which she lays her eggs. Then she covers them with a layer of silk. She wraps more silk around the bundle to make an **egg sac**.

The picture above shows a female spider making her egg sac. On the opposite page, you can see baby spiders hatching from their eggs inside the silken sac.

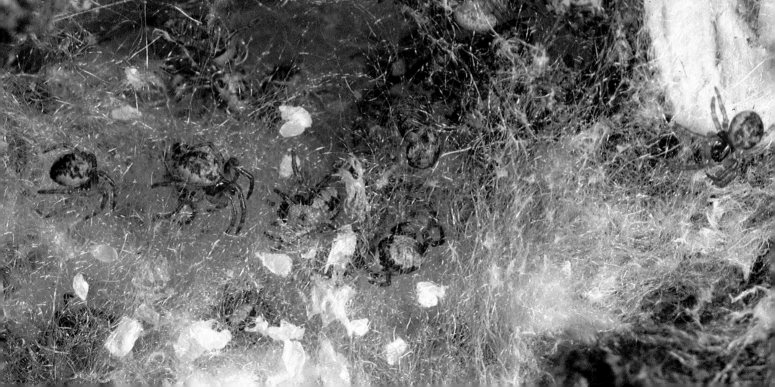

Argiope bruennichi

Female spiders make different kinds of egg sacs and take care of them in different ways. The black-and-yellow spider shown on the left makes a sac shaped something like a pitcher. Like many orb-web spiders, she hangs her egg sac on plant stems near her web and watches over it.

Other kinds of female spiders make special webs or shelters of silk in which they hide their egg sacs. A nursery-web spider (*Pisaura*) hangs her egg sac among leaves on a plant. Then she spins a web over the leaves to make a kind of silk tent. The mother spider stands guard over her nursery, waiting for the eggs to hatch.

After baby spiders, or **spiderlings**, come out of their eggs, they usually stay inside the egg sacs for some time. They have to finish their development before leaving the protection of the sac. Some female spiders, like *Crytophora* (opposite), stay with the egg sac until the spiderlings emerge. Other females leave or die before the young spiders emerge.

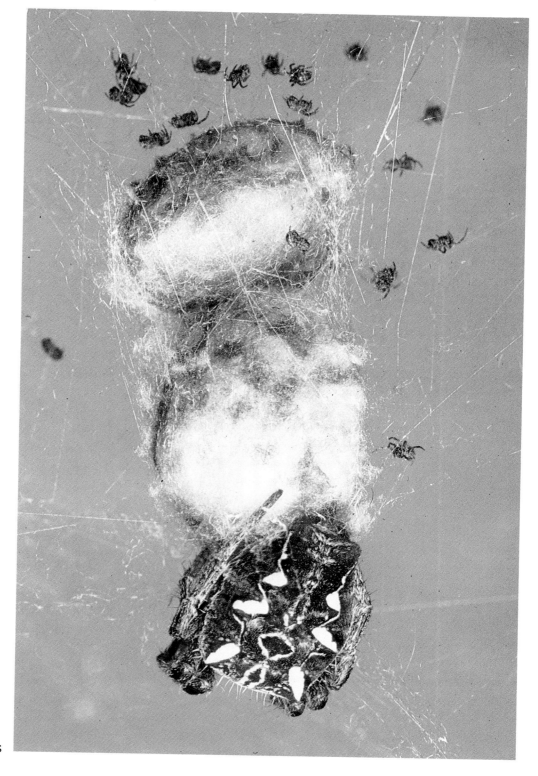

Crytophora species

Wolf spiders take unusually good care of their eggs and young. After making her egg sac, a female wolf spider (below) uses silk threads to attach it to her spinnerets. She will keep the sac with her until the eggs are ready to hatch.

During the day, wolf spiders sometimes stay in burrows in the ground. At night, they come out to look for insects. Whether a female is hiding underground

Lycosa tarentula. Body length about 1 inch (25 mm)

or running after prey, her egg sac stays attached to her body. It does not seem to get in her way.

When the baby wolf spiders have hatched from their eggs and are ready to leave the egg sac, the female helps them. She opens the tough silk of the sac with her claws. Out come the spiderlings, which look like tiny copies of their large mother (next page).

As soon as the wolf spiderlings get out into the world, they do a very strange thing. They run up their mother's legs and climb onto the top of her abdomen. Soon all the baby spiders, as many as 200 in some wolf spider species, are piled neatly on the female's back.

Once her passengers are on board, the female spider goes about her usual business. When she chases after prey, the babies come along for the ride. If they fall off, she waits until they run after her and scramble back up her legs. The spiderlings do not eat but live off the remains of their egg yolks, which are still inside their bodies.

The young wolf spiders will stay on their mother's back until they develop completely and can be on their own. This may take anything from a few days to several weeks, depending on the species of wolf spider.

In addition to the wolf spider, there are a few other spider mothers that provide care for their young. Some female comb-footed spiders (*Theridion*) feed their babies with a liquid from their mouths. When the young spiders get bigger, they share the prey that their mothers catch.

Some kinds of female spiders feed their babies with their own bodies. After her young hatch, a *Coelotes* female brings insects for them to eat. When she dies, the spiderlings get the nourishment they need by eating her body.

Many spiders, such as garden spiders and other orb-web weavers, do not care for their young. When the spiderlings leave the egg sac, they are on their own. The young spiders may stay together for a short time before going their separate ways.

Many young spiders leave the place of their birth by a special method called **ballooning**. A ballooning spider climbs up to a high place and sends out a thread of silk. The thread floats in the breeze and eventually lifts the spider into the air. Carried by the wind, it may land in a spot where it can begin its life as an adult. On their journeys to new homes, however, many ballooning spiders fall into water or are eaten by birds.

Lycosa tarentula

37

Araneus diadematus

Theraphosa leblondi. Body length about 3½ inches (about 9 centimeters). Leg span up to 10 inches (25 cm).

A process called **molting** is an important part of every young spider's development. When a spider molts, it sheds the hard outer covering of its body.

Like insects, spiders do not have an internal skeleton. Instead, they have an outer skeleton, or **exoskeleton**, that protects the soft parts of their bodies. This hard covering does not grow as a young spider grows. From time to time, it must be replaced by a larger exoskeleton that develops underneath it.

The photograph on the opposite page shows an old exoskeleton that has been shed by a garden spider. You can see that the top part of the cephalothorax is raised up like the lid of a box. The spider got out of the old exoskeleton through the split between the upper and lower parts of the body.

In the picture above, a large bird spider has wiggled its body out of the old exoskeleton. Now it must get its eight legs out of the old covering. This is a big job, something like a human taking off tight stockings or tall boots.

A large spider like the bird spider may take several hours to pull its long legs out of the old exoskeleton (upper left). During this time, it cannot run or defend itself from any predator that might attack.

When a spider finishes molting, its new exoskeleton is completely developed but pale and soft. It will gradually darken and become hard. Before the exoskeleton hardens, the spider expands its body to stretch the new covering. This will make room for further growth. At the same time, the spider bends and stretches its legs so that the joints do not become stiff as the new exoskeleton hardens.

All young spiders molt several times during their early period of growth. Once they become adults, most spiders do not need to molt because they do not get any bigger. There are some large spiders, however, that live long lives and continue to grow. The bird spider is one of these spiders, which scientists call **mygalomorphs** (MY-gah-loh-morfs). In North America, these large, hairy spiders are commonly known as tarantulas.

Bird spiders can live up to 20 years and usually molt once or twice a year as adults. Smaller spiders like the garden spider or the jumping spider live for no more than one year.

Gasteracantha species

The common spiders of North America and northern Europe are generally quite small. Most very large spiders like the bird spider live in South America and other tropical parts of the world. *Nephila*, the golden silk spider (opposite page), is a large orb-web weaver that lives in warm climates. As much as 2 inches (5 centimeters) in length, this beautiful spider makes a huge web out of yellow silk. The silk is so strong that, in some tropical countries, people use its threads to make nets for fishing.

Other tropical spiders are noted not for their size but for their bright colors and unusual shapes. Less than 1/2 inch (12 millimeters) long, the spiny-bodied spiders shown on the left have brilliantly colored abdomens with spikes and spines sticking out of them.

Large or small, bright in color or plain, spiders are fascinating animals. Look for them among the plants in your garden or in dark corners inside your house. If you watch closely as they spin their webs or wait for prey, you might even come to admire these amazing eight-legged creatures.

Nephila species

Araneus cucurbitinus

Araneus quadratus (above and below)

THE NAMES OF SPIDERS

The names of spiders can be very confusing. Many spiders, even common ones, do not have names in English. Other eight-leggers may have several different English names. For example, the garden spider shown on the opposite page is also known as the cross spider because of the cross-shaped markings on its abdomen. But this spider has only one scientific name: *Araneus diadematus.* The name identifies the spider's genus and species, two groups in the system of scientific classification. It is written in Latin so that it can be understood by people all over the world, no matter what language they speak.

The three spiders shown on the left are close relatives of the garden spider, as you can see from their scientific names. They belong to the same genus —*Araneus*—but are members of two different species.

In this book, we have given the genus or species name of all the spiders shown. When a spider has a familiar and accepted English name, we have used it as well.

GLOSSARY

abdomen: the rear section of a spider's body, containing the reproductive organs and silk glands

arachnids: members of the scientific class Arachnida. Spiders, mites, ticks, daddy longlegs, and scorpions belong to this group.

ballooning: a method of travel in which spiders float through the air on threads of silk

bridge thread: the first thread of an orb web, on which the rest of the web is built

cephalothorax: the front section of a spider's body, made up of the head and thorax, or chest

chelicerae: appendages on a spider's cephalothorax used to catch and kill prey. The singular form of the word is **chelicera.**

dragline: a silk safety line that spiders attach to objects as they move from place to place

egg sac: the silk container that a female spider spins around her eggs

exoskeleton: the hard covering that protects the soft parts of a spider's body

funnel web: a web with a sheet of silk at the top and a funnel-shaped section at the bottom

genus: a group in the system of scientific classification made up of two or more species

instinct: an ability or behavior that is inherited rather than learned

molting: shedding an old exoskeleton

mygalomorph: a spider whose chelicerae move up and down rather than from side to side as in other spiders. The large spiders known in North America as tarantulas belong to this group.

orb webs: round webs with a spiral pattern

palps: appendages on the cephalothoraxes of spiders. The palps of male spiders have enlarged chambers at the ends that are used to hold sperm.

predators: animals that kill and eat other animals

prey: animals that are killed and eaten by predators

sheet web: a flat, horizontal spider web

signal thread: a thread of silk connecting a spider to its web. Vibrations of the signal thread tell the spider that an insect is caught in the web.

species: the basic group in the system of scientific classification, made up of animals with many common characteristics

sperm: male reproductive cells. The union of male sperm cells with female egg cells produces new individuals.

spiderlings: baby spiders

spinnerets: the fingerlike tubes at the end of a spider's abdomen through which silk emerges from the body

INDEX

abdomen, 8
arachnids, 7
Araneus, 11, 44
Argiope, 17, 27

baby spiders. *See* spiderlings
ballooning, 36
bird spider, 39, 40, 41, 42
bridge thread, 12, 14

cephalothorax, 8, 39
chelicerae, 9, 24
Coelotes, 36
comb-footed spiders, 36
crab spiders, 7, 22, 24
cross spider, 44
Crytophora, 18, 30

dragline, 23

eggs, 28, 30, 32, 33
egg sacs, 28, 30, 32, 33, 36
exoskeleton, 39, 40
eyes, 9
eyesight, 21, 23, 27

fangs, 9, 21, 24
fear of spiders, 5
feeding habits, 21, 24, 35, 36
funnel webs, 19

garden spiders, 11, 36, 39, 41, 42, 44
golden silk spider, 42
growth of spiders, 39, 41

houses, spiders in, 5, 19
hunting spiders, 7, 22-23, 27

jumping spiders, 7, 23, 27, 41

legs, 7, 8, 39, 40

mating, 27-28
molting, 39-41
mygalomorphs, 41

names of spiders, 44
Nephila, 42
nursery-web spiders, 30

orb web, 7, 11, 17, 42; making of, 12-14
orb-web spiders, 14, 17, 21, 30, 36, 42

palps, 27
poison, 5, 9, 21, 22, 23
predators, spiders as, 7, 9, 21, 22-23

sheet webs, 18
signal thread, 21
silk, 7, 8, 21, 23; used in egg sac, 28; used in webs, 12-14, 17, 18-19, 42
spiderlings, 28, 30; care of, by mother, 30, 33-35, 36
spinnerets, 8, 12
spiny-bodied spiders, 42

tarantulas, 41
Tegenaria, 19
tropical regions, spiders in, 42

webs, 7, 27; funnel, 19; as insect traps, 18, 21; orb, 7, 11, 12-14; sheet, 18; used in mating, 27
wolf spiders, 7, 27, 32-35

ABOUT THE AUTHOR

Claudia Schnieper began her career as a book seller and is now a free-lance writer, editor, and translator. She is the author of several nature books for children, including the Carolrhoda Nature Watch books *On the Trail of the Fox* and *An Apple Tree through the Year.* Claudia lives with her husband, Robert, various cats and dogs, and a parrot in an old farmhouse near Lucerne, Switzerland.

ABOUT THE PHOTOGRAPHER

Max Meier is a free-lance photographer who specializes in photographing animals. When he is not busy taking pictures of spiders, frogs, and chameleons, he works in the Veterinary Hospital in Zurich, Switzerland. Max has published several animal books for children and an adult book on amphibians and reptiles. He makes his home in Zurich.